The Radiant

The Radiant

Lise Goett

ISBN-13: 978-1-961209-15-2
Library of Congress Control Number: 2024945265

Design by Howard Klein

Cover Photograph: Geraint Smith. "Ranchito Road Snows." Private collection.
Used by permission of the artist.

First paperback edition December 2024.

Tupelo Press
P.O. Box 1767
North Adams, Massachusetts 01247
(413) 664-9611 / Fax: (413) 664-9711
editor@tupelopress.org / www.tupelopress.org

Tupelo Press is an award-winning independent literary press that publishes fine fiction,
non-fiction, and poetry in books that are a joy to hold as well as read. Tupelo Press is a
registered 501(c)(3) non-profit organization, and we rely on public support to carry out
our mission of publishing extraordinary work that may be outside the realm of the large
commercial publishers. Financial donations are welcome and are tax deductible.

CONTENTS

—For Nathan Filbert and Alden Borders, "The Bookmen"

There is a time when you can no longer say, my God.

—Carlos Drummond de Andrade

After a Dark Tunnel, Uplift, Lift

Bliss,

we are not separate   but one   with snow.

The firs   caught in an updraft   are

raising their tails,

revelers   in the undersides of things,

spiritii and *spiritelli*

held back for a time

by a wind   in high dudgeon—

on and off   all day

not yet yielding—

fleet daemons

suspended   in   *maybe*

it will snow.

It will snow—

the air   snow-flecked,

hackled   in high bluster

& on its Way.

Lo,

these white specks,   morsellings

above a sky ballroom without ceiling,

the world unmasking   a dream.

But whose dream is it—

God's

or the tumors'—   they, too, flurrying,

on and off,

attention hovering where the world was,

above an ashen cloud,

flecks of emulsion,   of recognition.

(O, this is *that* dream.

What has happened that I cannot escape it?)

I must say

I have enjoyed   Time,

the eternal, the immortal supply—

bubbles ascending,

a mirror ball throwing sparks inside a luminous glass—

the cancer everywhere—

in a whoosh   of gold flooding,

the mountainside

on the cusp of   chartreuse—

radiant cells lost in whiteout, in whorl,   a mute murmuration of bees

(Surely bees must have little feet for burrowing-in, for sleep in honeyed winter),

this vesseling body, the cove of my bed, the work

I do from it,   swooped for,   snatched out of the mouth

of oblivion   as from a hunter's snare.

*

Alas, I am writing   to tell you   I must decline

your beautiful invitation.

I shall be attending to snow   and burrowing.

But to miss your   beautiful   table

and   your pudding

which is   rarer,   to die for.

Excuse me,   the new drug.

I am sure it decimates boundaries—the truth

of the end   a fiction

polished to a high gloss   I cannot speak of.

But

as you can   hear, I won't   be able

to   come.   I have accepted an invitation that starts at 5.

I will be limp   by 7,

as white as a ghost,

hovering over the white dream where the world was,

a ballroom without ceiling—

I a dandelion's spent head become the specular image,   a mere spirit

of the body blown out to some new seeding, some lovely asunder:

an iron filing drawn in the magnet's attraction   to the bliss of flesh called astonishment,

uplifted

in awe

& like a murmuration of bees,   of snow,

                                        fleet daemon of the air, this life

                        passes, is passed.

I

Difficult Body

There is a time, in the mind, when the soul slips
from its cerement and goes to live like a fruit bat in the rafters,
flying through the ether like no real bird, knowing no bounds,

and, fey little wanderer that it is, watches from above—
as in a surgical theater—the bodies of all things being born into this world
under a sign of error,
of negation, as they are being erased.

*

*Inhibited in their aims, the emotional impulses
torque into aberration*, divide and multiply
like cells seeking a new host.

You could be eighteen again, watching your stand-in, your stunt double—
a sherbet Frankenstein in waitress uniform, serving pancakes
and pots of hot coffee, smiling for the customer,
but inside, you burned *like a fire shut in stone.*

How could you help
but become magma, enigma?

When did it come, the split, the Others,
the voice asking, *What of your shining body revealed?*
It was only a matter of time
before your psyche separated from the body
like a blister.

*

It is then that the soul returned to the heyday of childhood,
its boneyard of linoleum

speckled like an oyster catcher's egg—
that reliquary of slide rules and dead languages,
pink sugar cubes soaked in vaccine,
Our Lady of Good Counsel,
where the hard discipline of the Sisters
tried to forge you into God's Marine.

*

You clapped erasers and cleaned chalkboards, incensed yourself
in the ambergris of chalk, in a talcum of smoke, cocooned, you thought,
in a happy childhood, until you were told that you don't remember.

*

It hadn't happened yet, the disaster's fallout like manna or ground
pumice or gray flotsam. You simply practiced the drills,
filing past the Glass Wax stencils of snowflakes and bulletin boards,

*

drinking the milk of amnesia, crouching under wooden desks,
memorizing the cadence of your own diaphragm rising and falling,
anklets neatly tucked under the buttocks,

*

back curled like unshelled shrimp—all that abundance of pink flesh—
pre-sexual—so vulnerable that the predator wanted to mar it,
gelid and available, steal its energy, capture it for his own private use,

*

the soul's little light doused out for the air raid.

Free Fall

Lately you've been in a fugue state,
travelling from terminal to terminal,
hoping to be met at the gate,

a glory ago since your father met you,
NYT tucked under his arm,
he ready to carry you, your bags,

his jacket suffused with half of your DNA,
a musk that spelled *home*.
Who now comes out of nowhere to save you?

Window shutter lowered at half-mast,
a glint of wingtip banking through cloud,
an attendant passes through

with emerald-green miniatures of Tanqueray,
lights orchestrated to dim as at a planetarium.
Your seatback reclined like a Barcalounger,

a tray table presses into your gut
from the recumbent passenger in front of you.
These are your teachers, so say the Buddhists,

those gadflies sent to make you grow.
Learn to picnic in a war zone, says the bodhisattva,
strapped in as you are for the convenience

of the attendants who disappear
with your credit card, bring back more snacks
and samples of oblivion.

Knowledge is rest, rest knowledge.
God, the Void, will keep you safe in the Turbulences,
a Venus-flytrap mask deployed from its compartment

when the cabin pressure drops.
Science now says that the sluffed cells
you left in your mother's womb

have the power to heal,
each of us restored by the spoke-light of another's radiance.
Breathe in, breathe out, little galaxy, little bundle of cure.

Might we suppose that everyone suffers
from some variety of private madness,
that we're sitting armrest to armrest,

madness to madness, seatback to seat,
life resembling a coffin-suite for contortionists,
your seatmate snoring—

you in your own placental, spacesuit pod,
tethered by a vacuum-hose umbilical?
You hope to remain attached to your allotment

of recycled air—even to take it all—floating around
but never really able to leave the womb, your fetal attitudes
or your dependence on air, on mother ship.

Tray top stowed, seat in the upright position,
you now wish you had listened more attentively.
In case of emergency landing over water,

the nearest exit may be behind you.
The flight is getting a little bumpy.
The pilot, you learn, bailed out long ago,

was voted off the craft, in fact,
and now the Yoda in cruise-director, Hawaiian shirt
is directing everyone to sing *Kumbaya*.

Do you need to clobber him with your big, black handbag
that carries everything—the diapers,
the baby food, the first-aid kit, the load—

your pathetic, mothering hope?
The attendant pushing the galley cart piled
with little silver trays reminds you, you had choices

before you booked this flight.
Choose nothing. Refusal is the first stage of passivity.
Or now that you're on board, you can always bail ship,

falling from the sky like one of those dead, yellow birds
who've forgotten how to migrate, the gadflies pecking
at your Hugh-Hefner-in-smoking-jacket stance as you descend.

Choose your entree, says the attendant. You wanted
to learn something about others' suffering, your greed?
It seems a glory ago your father met you at the gate.

And you want to be greeted by him,
with all your old cats and dead relatives
feasting at the lambent table, the lucelence of eternity,
so you choose the third option, to endure.

How to Avoid a Snake

You're right. There is a story here.
Perhaps you sense it.
It will take some excavation.
Let's agree to meet
over a plate of clams
at Cal Pep in Barcelona,
those tender bivalves
saucered in fragile shells,
translucent as the tips of fingers
or teardrops rinsed in daylight,
and there I promise to tell you the story.
You're the only person
to whom I will ever tell it.
I call it how to avoid a snake in the dark.
Because just to meet you there
will mean that we've escaped.
Perhaps we'll stumble, stunned
at having rinsed ourselves
in *jouissance* into the day's white pulse,
thinking that happiness, like beauty,
was something only to be seen
in arrears. We'll make a little roof
over our brows with our hands
to shield ourselves,
we who have lived
in the dark a long time,
until our eyes adjust
to luminosity
for even happiness hurts
a little.

What's the recipe for happiness, Maestro—
you who always speak of perfect practice,

the notes, the proper fingering,
the liquor that flesh yields,
that we'll sup from the same pan?
Is it the sweetness of the sherry,
the salt of the diced *jamon*?
It is then I will tell you the story
of how to avoid a snake.

Because we know a lot about the subject.
What's the antivenin for falling in love?
Will we administer it in time? My young friend
can't tell you what a snake sounds like crossing dry hardpan,
but she knows the click of an empty gun barrel
to her head. And there's the model with the S-scar.
She can't remember her stalker's face,
but she knows his tread. She can hear a footfall
better than my dog. After enough time,
one no longer stops for a stranger
on the roadside or for love. We move on.
In the dark the senses adjust.
One learns to see—or is it *feel*—
a snake coiling to strike.
We don't court trouble anymore.
We're the lucky ones.
Your wife doesn't understand you.
Let's meet in Barcelona.
But if you don't come, I'll understand.
Those urges one never acts upon
rustle in the dark.

Current Weather, Whether

Da Zuang Hexagram 34 [Great Vigor]

> *Look at your phone as tool, not obligation. Would you walk around with a hammer in your pocket? You would pick up a hammer when you needed it. You would never be addicted or obligated to it. Use your phone like a hammer. Only pick it up when you need it.*
>
> —Ye West

Everything is unfathomable and thick.

You no longer know where anyone is. They call from a secret venue. Perhaps from inside a human womb, the sound of amniotic fluid swishing in the background; and when *they*—now neuter, singular, intermittently insisting upon plural identities within the singularity of one—return your call—which is almost never—chances are you will be disconnected or go immediately to voicemail. You hear the potential of something more than you—you, they, other—the sound of amniotic fluid swishing in the background, a gelatinous oyster flushing down a golden toilet.

*

A phone is a hammer. A hammer is a phone.
You have no obligation to answer it.
You, yourself, your cry for help, are all alone.

*

It does not enter his mind that he lives alone in the world. —John Cage

It does not enter that there is no *here*. It does not enter.
It.

17

The human egg. The mind.

*

It again.
It, an uninvited in, an in-truder!

*

Wherever or whenever the word *it* appears, it must be used three times in rapid succession. *It, it, it,* like a machine gun.

That should kill *it.*
Kill what?
It!
Haven't you been listening?

It is your own best listener.

*

Toll the mice. Advance three aces.

*

He feels nostalgic for the receiver. The wasp-waisted, candlestick telephone with a tethering umbilicus, a cord. Here, here (hear, hear) for the old days of the receiver, the candlestick telephone, before the weather became the whether, back when there was a *before.* Now there is only no, on, oh on, oh hon.

*

No one answers.
You think perhaps it's because you are calling from a hammer, not a phone.
You can't tell from where they are calling, from down the street or from
Bangalore.
—*They?*
You. Your electronic neighbors.

The passcode is inscrutable. (You can't remember. Indeed, you never have been
able to.)
Not after your aunt candled you like an egg when you were six (so small, so
vulnerable), the aunt who grew the giant cucumbers. She removed your Coke-
bottle glasses and turned you round and round as in a game of hide-and-seek.
That's when the fog moved in, the whether, and you became hysterically blind.
That's when you began to forget. Remember?

*

The neighbor's house alarm goes off at 5:53 a.m. every day.
They live a thousand miles away.

The autocorrect has turned *unacceptable* into *edible*.
Yes, these are just the everyday inconveniences. Cannibals

are watching from a promontory,
as in: *From a promontory, an Indian watched the Donner Party*

eat themselves. It is you who eat yourself.

Your neighbors are simply waiting until you're gone,
done.

*

Cannibals.

They don't exist. Haven't we established that?
Let's establish at least one thing. You are alone!

I reiterate: You are your own best listener.

*

It does not enter his mind that he lives alone in the world. —John Cage

*

Perhaps a *she* exists. Perhaps a *she* is lactating from inside the human egg.

You wave at the Abyss. The Abyss waves back.

And then the Abyss walks away and gives you the finger.

You thought that you had some proprietary claim on the Abyss?

*

Achtung. The Abyss is calling you from the placenta.

Can't you hear the heartbeat inside the human egg?
If so, pick up. Place your hand upon the receiver. Can you feel the fetus kick?
I am hanging up the hammer now. Farewell.

*

You married the goddess three times and each time the goddess left.
Try dialing this numb(er), later on, anon, at noon.

Someday, somewhere, you'll find someone younger,
younger enough to be a mirror to your own—

until—alas, alack, anon—you can't, you don't.
The mirror tarnishes; the goddess disappears.

*

A hammer is a phone, a phone is a hammer.

Clean cut as Mr. America on tour,
what happened to your star-spangled mind
strafing ruffian skies?
What does it mean
to say we have no state of emergency,
a black reduction of blood
pooling from your hammered head?
Someone came to martyr you.
You decide to scream.
No epitaph.

*

In the game of ruth and flare,
how is it that you always think you're *it?*

Cassandra's Curse

The house on Atlantic Avenue's windows
are barred now, the once paved
drive surrendered to weeds.

The neighborhood, once large and safe
to roam, has shown the wear of age—
like a stooped, old man, abandoned

but tied for safety to a clothesline:
no good way to end. *It's ugly now*, I say.
It was always ugly, my sister says.
I don't remember it that way.

The houses had Doric columns,
and the best of them, a stately
quality—reproductions of a grandeur

from the past, but now in midday,
everyone at work, the streets seem vacant,
run down. My sister, the official family

chronicler, tells me our mother changed
after I was born. Monday was always laundry day,
then everything went south.

*Four kids, one station wagon. Who wouldn't be
a little frazzled? Things happen. Hormones change.*
Every christening has its uninvited guest.

I don't remember it that way. I remember dance
classes at the Washington School of Ballet.
I remember whipping Denny Via with a honeysuckle vine.

I remember burning down the family tent
and how we made a sour mash of acorns
like the Assateagues who were forced to leave this place.

You got things I needed but didn't get.
You can never repay
me for what I did for you.

I took care of you. I protected you.
I don't remember it that way:
nothing menacing in the basement,

nothing dark beneath the bed. *Not so*, my sister said.
The hollow, evening air sometimes sways
with a wailing from somewhere deep inside the earth.

The felling of a tree, a rape, a massacre—
a child's cry, perhaps—prophesy
a curse. No one wants to hear my sister's voice.

Sinistra

It's just a Thursday night in the flatlands of America.
He sits down and orders an Old Fashioned. Clam rolls,
all you can eat. He tells the waitress that his brother
owns a restaurant in West Liberty. The brother's hiring.
He says that he wants to talk about it more but in another
place. Not this HoJo's. He'll wait for her until her end of shift.
He'll take her in his semi to the bar across the interstate.
His cab is warm, and the engine never stops
running. He worries the cherry in his drink. She glances at his hands:
not the hands of a man in a clean business, black crescents of motor oil
beneath his nails. She meets him in the hallway outside
the restaurant where some turn left, some right.
Such a simple decision, which way to go. He tells her she needs to go
with him. The sun is still out. It's summer. She vacates her body.
Her TV doppelganger tells him politely that she will drive
in her own car. She crosses the interstate and waits,
but he never shows. A light dusting of leaves on the pavement:
a preternatural fall before true autumn, the hard, rutted ground
with its cropped stubble where he might have thrown her down,
but he's long gone. His semi skims the highways, the susurrus
of tires on wet pavement. For years it haunts her, as she passes
every boarded-up façade, in every dying town, where there's nowhere
to go, not even for a spot of coffee. It haunts her, the missing eye
of that derelict bar, two towns over, gutted out. Dead, alive,
it's where she might have worked had she turned left instead of right.

The Voyeur

You like what is left unfinished,
 to visit the house where *here*
once was, a door now never opened
 but once left unlocked, this *here*
where you slipped without pretense
 or much preamble into her bed,
proffering your snuffling rut, carrying
 your seasons with you as animals do,
snout hoisted to the requiem of winter.

 It was the undoing you loved best,
the ceremonial unwrapping of her light cotton housecoat,
 the tongues of her sash slipped from their loops,
your hands in flight across her esophagus,
 instincts acting in tandem—
her gutteral writhe, her whimper of consent—
 obsession as endless as study itself.

She knows that you are still there
 shivering in the dark,
awaiting her nightly performance
 and delights in this catch and release,
the elaborate striptease and slip of her robe
 to the floor, playing exhibitionist to your voyeur,
her allure confirmed by violation.

Now you dance alone with the vodka
 you keep in the freezer to ease the duress
of living, the gutted hull of your days,
 oblivion conjured up from the decomposed
slops of the potato, remembering as you drink
 that the Spirit, too, is a phantom that can assail
a human with more force than flesh.

Your mind has grown tardy, never arriving,
whole provinces of memory ceding to blank plains.
Even the lake where pain lives is freezing over,
ice floes and black vines making these waters
impassible, your life fogbound in stagnant rehearsal,
the stars, their loneliness, impassive,
as you ride in a body not *here*.

II

The Muses

Entre chien et loup, two—no three—lithe figures appear,
distinctly female, accompanied by a retinue
of chalk-white hounds, threading in and out of the larches.

When my husband asks where I've been,
I do not pretend to tell the radiant specifics,
but he can smell the residues of their ravishing,

appraise the thumbprints rouged by feverish hands.
What man can match the silk of three?
He scrutinizes my flush, my vacant gaze,

how I blossom in anticipation of my evening guests,
or rush to watch a downpour glisten the burn pile,
earth within earth everywhere, there where the agapanthus

relinquishes its leaves. They come and go, unbidden.
In everything a little of them remains:
in the rosé tints at the crepuscular hour,

in the silt at lake's bottom, in the empty bowl that sings.
The Muses' carriage has not yet arrived.
No one has arrived. So leave me

as you would a dead one, with no regret.
Without knowing it, we are all waiting
for the Muses' carriage, carrying us, to arrive.

The Abduction

Blighted, yes, by days when nothing rose up.
These were *the war years*, I called them,
even though there was no war.

Be open, the voice said, its edges like water.
This resistance you feel, the world always wanting—
what of your shining body revealed?

All day, I watched swimmers
come back from the other shore,
golden, luminous skinned.
Moths made their little stairs
above the hydrangea,
tracing the strings of a lyre, played the song
of beautiful skin.

I wandered into the wood.
When the stag overcame me,
all roughshod and golden,
it was not human,
I an empty thing lifting up to the gorgeous,
gorged being above me.

In that moment, I am sure that I died,
my spirit unbound from its fascicle.

In April, I open
to the terrifying body that visits me.
The earth is red because I bleed.

I love him like pith
or the silk that leaves winged seeds, bell-tongued.
He alone is my habitat,

I blinded to sing the more sweetly,
my mind a fair copy of his,
imperceptible to the eye,
a whorl of thumbprint on the weir,
the scent of mimosa—haunted breath.

How to Get Pregnant

Among his many talents, Don Geraldo was a fine knitter of spells and a haruspex of entrails that sometimes revealed, in contradiction to all appearances, the subtext of a man's ambition. He possessed a grimoire—this is not to be confused with his codex of legends about angel helpers and mysterious pigeons found in the grain—but a book of charms, which he himself composed, to be sung first in the left ear, then into the right, then over the top of the head of whomever came to him wishing to exorcize dwarves or to cure a boil or to rid a field of bad sod.

One day, a man came to him who wished to be cured of an infestation of dwarves. Don Geraldo bade the inflicted man to abide in his purpose, for even defiled men do not want to reside in the filth of their own intentions, preferring a straw pallet with clean sheets to a manger. Don Geraldo then instructed the inflicted to ingest seven wafers, each inscribed with a name of one of the Seven Sleepers (Malchus, servant of Caiaphas, whose ear was severed by Peter, and so on), for seven consecutive days, and to ask a virgin to lie abed with him and sing, *A spider-thing came on the scene with his cloak in his hand, claiming you for his horse, and put his cord on your neck...* A poultice of yeast and honey, oil and milk was then hung around the neck, and this was repeated for three days in order to rekindle in the accursed a divine purity, a practice Don Geraldo maintained until there was a shortage of town virgins.

Don Geraldo then instructed the man to make and keep under his bedstead a pot of stew prepared from the middle digits of an animal, which were consubstantial, Geraldo claimed, with the relics of five saints kept under lock and key in a house on another continent. Said stew was also known to cure scrofula and worms. The next morning, the man found the pot licked clean and in its place five, long, human metatarsals. What remains is a mutilated story, best saved for telling on a snowy day when inviting neighbors over to dine on the windfall viands of a wolf attack.

Nine months later, as nature would have it, a baby was born to Don Geraldo's daughter, Amelia. No one knew by whom. The child was missing a middle toe. That night the *patrón* had a dream in which his daughter visited him in the form of a city undergirded and fretted with passageways, ossuaries, middens of broken bone, a grotto of radiant light. Much relieved by this omen, Don Geraldo christened the baby Luca, and taking credit as though he had given birth to the baby himself, after great effort, as God would, Don Geraldo slept.

Dirge

For Charcot, the arched body...the hysterical woman...is a subject of entertainment.
　　　—Louise Bourgeois

Direct my way—for *dirge*
is a womanly direction—
lathed by tongues—burned at stake—
an imperative

etched in fire—as women are—
by walk of shame
for comely wild, the Master's stave—
aimed to split our music—

what we call our laundry song—
for what's run through the mangle—
indentured—forced to grub
the jewels of gentle men—

to Kingdom come—
the vixen treed—
hounds rounding the ash-
heap of women martyred—

Play our funeral march at font—beg ablution
for the died-in-childbirth.
Belfried, arched, deemed hysterical—
we set the manse on fire—

the Master maimed—
we the only poets left
in the hermitage. *Blaze, Jane—*
for the rest of life is prose.

The Summit Will Teach You

—Sir Edmund Hillary (July 20, 1919 - January 11, 2008)

How ironic it is to greet you here
from sea level, dear Tenzing,

to announce my final ascent,
dozing here at the Oriental Hotel

in the arms of a rattan cobra,
awakened by a snap

of a waiter's linen napkin dropped in my lap,
while in West Bengal frets of cloud sow

in the hummocks between the steep, green tea rows
of Darjeeling, porters hunkering in the one hut

the one vowel of indivisible breath,
rain's rampant timpani in the slop bucket,

faces lit by the pith of one rushlight dipped in tallow
in those high, green valleys of the Shar Pa.

Imagine at my age, the thin air, the brain deprived
of oxygen, evaporating into the cloud rest of nonbeing!

An aborigine once told me that I
had no business walking on the spine

of the Mother Goddess.
How could I feign my heart innocent

of the setup, deny the nature of the skin
I was born into?

Wouldn't the earth be better without us?
The summit will teach you, you said.

Having summited that day in May,
you did not know how to operate the camera.

Lowe greeted us in base camp with hot soup.
We knocked that bastard down, I said.

I write you to make this late apology.
I am old now and not good for much anymore,

but I count it the greatest privilege simply to have lived
and known you. How diminutive life seems

viewed now from the great height of the summit:
the narrow-gauge railway connecting Darjeeling

to the plains, a toy constructed
for the summering colonials to compare

the ostinato of crickets meting out the temperature,
the legato of their circadian clocks,

with their thrum back home.
This elaborate effort to name the world and pin it down,

our crampons and silken parachutes,
the paraphernalia of our ambition hauled to the top,

glacier-blue, anoxic,
we who are finite, cruciform, arrive,

run out of water, air, time
in our pursuit of clear communion

with infinitude, this dazzling air we breathe
our dying sarcophagus,

counting the corpses we pass on our way down.

How to Plant Corn

During the years the townspeople euphemistically called Don Geraldo's bewilderment, an unsaddled donkey wandered into the old man's courtyard, a beast who came into his possession through the power of prayer. Consequently, he christened the donkey with the name Belief. Because he often left the donkey tied to a railing in the *praça* and forgot where he had last left the animal, Don Geraldo could often be seen walking through the village in his nightgown and slippers, crying out like a self-made muezzin: *Where is my Belief?*—Geraldo, haruspex, summoning the faithful.

Geraldo's addled state commenced shortly after his wife's death in a fire thought to have been begun by a group of professional arsonists, but it is equally plausible that the fire was begun by his neighbor, Osvaldo Alonso, who actually owned the donkey. The flames turned his wife's platinum necklace mauve and, with the exception of her right arm (which had been preserved by the hard carapace of a valise she had been packing), left her entire body charred—a cruciform skeleton adorned with a single ornament. Even in waking, the dreams of old age ghosted beneath the surface of Don Geraldo's consciousness like a herd of beluga whales, the buffalo of the ocean, who suckle upon the frozen crust of winter sea in search of oxygen. Sometimes the arm appeared to him out of nowhere in his dreams, an opera glove made of flesh minus the face of his beautiful wife. Once he awoke, proclaiming that he had slept with a frosty king, and, in exchange, the king had promised to give him a master sack of corn. The next day, it snowed. Thinking the snow seed corn from heaven, he gathered the first frost crop in buckets and had his plow blessed by a parish priest. Even after Don Geraldo's death, his field yielded a crop that no living hand had ever planted. Some even said that in his stead one could see an amiable angel guiding the plow and oxen from behind.

One night, a band of hooligans roused him out of bed and clothed him in the habit of a nun. They said nothing of or to him but blindfolded him and turned him about three times as in a child's game and, not wishing to deny him the adventure, sent him out on the road alone. The next day, the townspeople marveled that he had been found some great distance away on the mountain, sitting beneath the sign of the Cross, where he had assembled a cave out of stones to enclose "the mouth of idle gossip." When asked how he made it over the treacherous terrain blindfolded, he said that he had chased a wild goose there for quill and a hand had reached out of the depths to steady him—a missive from the other side in its most immortal and tenuous traces. It is not enough to follow an idea to its end, he said. One must feel the dreamer dreaming oneself, and in this certainty, in perilous times, allow oneself to drift.

Apologia for Hermeticism

—For Paul Celan

As through a stag's larynx whose throat
was never meant for speech, you speak

notes forced through pipes that choke breath back,
air rife with the vapor-rags God throws down at twilight,

an ingot lodged inside you,
soliloquizing to the shadows that pool

in unnumbered graves,
a strange fruit plucked from air

to appease a mother ghost no one sees nor names
where the dead lie in sundry postures of ordination,

o no one, o you, an almond-eyed mentor of bitters,
a David who put his sling down, you speak

despite the dregs of living, you speak
among the silences we teach ourselves to ruin,

teetering on the precipice of oblivion
an oath of God to God's satisfaction.

Hildegard

[Hildegard of Bingen was a 12th-century visionary and mystic who saw "The Shade of the Living Light," her visions recorded in the book of Scivias. These visions caused her great suffering and tribulation.]

I

As a child with migraines,
an affliction from God,
you saw the wheeling of a bright city above you,
a town on the outskirts of vision, without bells,

the fontanelle's damp parapet the first to touch dawn,
the craniumed, crinolined brain split like an eggshell.

You thought yourself lost in a citadeled town,
the first pain—God's lobation—coming like the pressing
of a book in the hand,
its hieroglyphs in a secret script you'll never decipher.

II

Yellow custard light, the pizzicato of water
falling like beads in the cistern. Black-eyed girls
crowd in the doorway to watch you,
their buff-colored skin the color of plunder.

III

At the city's nine gates:
apostles, anvils,
splayed racks for drying elk,
the pelts of red owls,
corn necklaces strung like abacuses of sleep—
the mustard seed of God's commerce,
and beyond: an exhalation of field.

IV

The sweat of cold limestone.
The hand pressing the wall is not yours.
Not the bone comb but what time harrows.
God is your habitat, you an emptied, disembodied thing
lifting up to the godhead rustling inside you,
the spirit unhinged from its fascicle.

V

Who is not vespertine, blossoming in evening,
the golden hind of this city
slipping down to slake their thirst,
the river's glossy brilliantine the color of aspens
already changing high in the mountains?

The spirits who wander these paths of crushed talus even step lightly.
They are lighting their lamps, the color of evening
as you wander the vespine galleries of this Alhambra
where the farther you go
the more you are lost,
the child you once were,
snared in the web of an invisible city.

VI

Pain sighs day into release,
the lemon grove's resins expressing their odor,
the limp weight of bedclothes—some Pietà.
God as your ravener.

VII

Take up your anchor and sing.

Codicil

If you want to go further, the voice said,
you will have to go back to the Beginning,
to the one hundred & twenty five acres of land
bequeathed to Elizabeth Lynn, the Belle of Nebo,
once bounded as follows to wit:

Beginning at two dogwoods two ashes & one white oak in original line
& also corner to Judith Jones running South 100 poles

to a small hickory & three dogwoods thence West 194 poles

to three Elms & hickory thence then North 100 poles

to an Elm Sassafras & black walnut then East 194 poles

to the Beginning

And the one hundred and twenty five acres given to his daughter Judith Jones was
bounded as follows to wit.

Beginning (at three black gums at an elbow in a lane defined by trees), running
with original line (clearly line) South 105 poles to two dogwoods two ashes &
white oak in said line thence West 194 poles to an
Elm Sassafras & black Walnut thence North 102 poles to a poplar & hickory
thence East 194 poles to the beginning

To Mariah Prunty one hundred dollars

To Susan Newbrough fifty dollars and a negro girl during her life but she is to
have no further part

To Delilah Littlepage nothing
To Julia Ann Hardesty nothing

I give and bequeath however to my grand daughter Elizabeth H Kelly daughter of my son John Kelly a negro girl named Susan now about one year old to her and her heirs forever

This 14th Dec'r 1855 Fred Kelly

1 Small Table	1.25
1 Bed & Stead & furniture	15.00
1 Flax wheel	3.00
5 chairs	2.00
1 Bureau	10.00
1 Dressing Glass	1.50
1 Small Table	3.00
1 lot of planes	1.00
2 chopping axes and sprouting hoe	1.50
60 bushels wheat	75.00
1 iron tooth harrow	3.00
1 Wagon & gear	35.00
1 buggy and harness	40.00
1 plow	5.00
3 hay stacks	25.00
30 acres growing corn	120.00
20 hogs	100.00
13 sheep	16.25
1 speckled cow and calf	12.00
4 yearlings	14.00
1 sorrel horse	90.00
1 mule	90.00
1 Negro man Sam	1100.00
1 Negro man Anthony	1200.00
1 Negro woman Clarissa	450.00
1 negro woman Caroline	1100.00
1 Negro boy Oliver	800.00
1 Negro girl Sarah	1050.00

*

In the 1880 census, I, Elizabeth Server nee Alexander
was age 80, living with my widowed son, Enoch Server
   with this notation next to my name,   (~~can neither read nor write.~~)

My male children are sawyers,
my husband, also a sawyer

                          (~~two dogwoods two ashes & one white oak~~)

   died of consumption.   (See Mortality Schedule appended here.)

     their flatboat hewn from timbers   (~~three elms & black walnut & hickory~~)

taken down

the Mississippi

River,

walking back, on foot

by the Natchez Trace,

these sawyers, my sons.

(~~To the Beginning~~).

*

If you are to go further, the voice said,
the current must take you there, the god of it, history,
choked with your secrets, roiling.

Today you are two.

Today you kill your father, become him,
taking your mother to bed,
return as the king,
father of what is dead,
that canal you passed through
into breath,
the den of comfort, the limp snake.

Free and secular, what now are you king of?

You stand in this lethal place,
the center point of a compass radiating outward,
its dial a stone-cutting blade,
your mother now pregnant.
What shall we call her?

You were pierced from the time
you left these four walls
with the thorns of the cholla,
by your seed
sickened,
bound on each side by a mountain.

Write this: *My ancestors cut down the virgin wilderness,*
plowed it with a backhoe,
sold it downriver.
I have lived five lives.
Write this: *Beneath this there is another life*
I am diving for, she whom I used to be.
How shall we count me? Her?
As one or as two?

As wind or as earth;
some ones are plural,
neither male nor female,
robbed of your mystery, your history a secret.
You stand in this place,
the center point of a compass
radiating outward.

From the east blows an ill wind,
pleating you like an accordion.
You'd have gills,
if you could speak,
touching her where your pact with mother earth
is unspoken, taboo,
taking her to bed.
The truth of what it can no longer hold back.

It's ruby season. Taste the fruit of the tiny, spined cholla.
They rise in coils of tumult, the covey of quail,
the ingle cold, the fire dead.

You wandered from your mother,
the river choked with what you asked it to hide
all these years, and carry away what needs to be said.
The god of grains: the amaranth and rapeseed—
on the side of the road
green cholla, its spiny hypodermics.
Back to the Beginning.

You have forgotten them, king.
Marry your mother, then take to your father's bed, your forgotten mother.
Not Zeus, not the small, green clocks of the cholla:
the river gods,
the river gods choked
with what can no longer be left
hidden. Choked down.

All those innocents caught in the stirrup
of the canyon and massacred.
What you destroy: a glittering track
pressed for oil by extreme heat
without the presence of oxygen.

To the east, an ill wind
carrying the scent of the creosote,
petrochemical silt from the shale mine.

Out of its mouth
blows the wind of the unlucky ones
from the east;
to the west, sun kilns the road.
To the south, concentration camps—
the bestial where, with
immensity,
the incarcerated
are beaten with the water of wands,
and the small gods of the cholla pierce,
secular and free,
until they are not, cannot:

three black gums at an elbow in a lane
(clearly a lane once defined by trees) running with original line (clearly line) South
105 poles to two dogwoods two ashes & white oak in said line thence West 194 poles
to an Elm Sassafras & black Walnut thence North 102 poles unfurling the
wands of water to a poplar & hickory
thence East 194 poles to the beginning   This 14th Dec'r 1855 Fred Kelly
two dogwoods, two ashes, one white oak gone. A small hickory, three elms, and three
black gums gone

until the pillars that hold up the sky crumble.

III

Wabi-Sabi

In the Hasui woodcut that hung above my childhood,
November rains in. *Wabi*: blossoming; *sabi*, decay.

Wabi once meant the misery of living alone, sabi: chill.
Over time, the meaning became entwined
with the beauty of the imperfect:
the chipped cup,
the fluorite-green ring around a maroon bruise,
or the fruit of the persimmon,
inedible until nearing decay.

*

In the Hasui woodcut, a woman leads a boy by the hand
through a courtyard of persimmon trees
toward the dank warmth of an outbuilding.

Perhaps this is farewell.
Perhaps she will not return.
Perhaps in minutes they will join the boy's father
over the steam of a soup made
with bok choy and a good broth.
We don't know how the story will end.
What needs to be said often waits.

*

In November, the chill monsoons already come,
my father took me to hear Caballé.
I don't remember which opera she sang.
Perhaps it was *Madame Butterfly*,
the libretto of a broken heart
and wabi: the misery of living alone.
At intermission, my father whisked me to the mezzanine
for Irish coffees served in upward, opening glasses fluted
with whipped cream, quickly drained

for the sweetest part, the demerara syrup
at the bottom of the glass.

My father's soul waited
until my sister's plane touched down on the tarmac,
rain coming down in the hospital courtyard.
She could not bear to see him die.
She could not walk through the door
until he turned white like the face of a Geisha
painted in the rice-powder makeup of moonlight
shed over a courtyard of persimmons in rain.
Wabi: blossoming; *sabi*: decay.

In Buddhism, the persimmon stands for transformation;
six signify enlightenment.
In the Hasui, there are only five.

The orange-red gobbets of flesh hang
from the skeletal branches, stripped of everything
but their fruit hearts, skin soon to be torn
by waxwings. On his deathbed, my father awaited his sixth.

Festina Lente

—after Susan Stewart

You must lie down now, for it is *you* who are vanishing,
not the forest. (It will remain here long after you're gone.)
Festina lente, hurry slowly, as if stalking a hen,
one you must catch from behind and hold tightly,
or it will run, thinking you a wolf, and not to be

returned home, to the coop, the hen startled to find herself alive.
You should sit down now, for it is *you* who are vanishing
at the writing desk set with your mother's brass candlesticks.
Festina lente, hurry slowly, as if stalking a hen.
Take in everything as if for the last time, your smell heightened,

for it is the sense of things invisible approaching, come to inhabit you for a time,
returned home, to the coop, the hen startled to find herself alive,
in spite of disfigurement, the halo of innocence that scourged you still shining.
At the writing desk, set with your mother's brass candlesticks,
you will find yourself—not the life you imagined but the beauty that lived you—

skin powdered white with ashes cupped in a gold compact,
of things invisible approaching, come to inhabit you for a time,
the yes and the no, the gurry and the gambol, held equally,
in spite of disfigurement, the halo of innocence that scourged you still shining.
You should lie down now in a field of narcissus,

a queen of Hades, your bodice left open for the dead,
skin powdered white with ashes cupped in a gold compact,
their mysterium strangering in you, impregnating you for a time,
the yes and the no, the gurry and the gambol, held equally—
as if you, yourself, were the only one who really knew how to hold you,
the truth of life always seen in arrears, in dusk's flat light,
a queen of Hades, your bodice left open for the dead

who suckle a blue runnel from your breasts, their colostrum,
their mysterium strangering in you, impregnating you for a time,
startled to return home, to the coop, still alive in the quickening.

Eros Addresses Psyche

I

Now that you are barren, now that you
are the messenger descending, making
your little stair into earth, light
on the crypt floor prefiguring the day
when you, too, will be lowered, your mor-
tifications too small to be of use—
wiping silt from the roost,
collecting eggs, your crown now packed in excelsior—
count yourself the favorite of the gods because
you survived your own abandon, never
to marry a fool who lies in a sanatorium,
drooling in a bib, his mind curdled on wine.
You will never know what you've been spared
until you are not. Even then you knew:
A man who only visits in the dark is dangerous.

II

Soul, it has been a long time
since I have visited you in the dark,
the nimbus of my breath left upon your neck
as seal of my dominion. I, a lord, gracious
and kind, am guilty of one crime, never to age,
while you listen to the pulleys of the grave
creak, wait for your time. Old age has stiffened
you in its waxen shroud, cast you like
an oyster shell upon a midden. You hear
no music, but I have not abandoned you,
only left you for a time. When the grass
is wet, it is I, Eros, who enter you.

III

Do you remember how we traveled to Hades
by skiff, cutting the motor? You were young
then and thought all virtues contained within
the god. Then doubt entered, and you lit
the lamp to see me as I really am.
Now you ride the wheat of white hands, buoyant
on wordlessness. And the coffin that floats
in your sleep, that knows you by name, without
speaking, has begun to inhabit your days,
How often I wanted to say: *In the cast of winter wheat,*
see the red tint of my wing descending. Meet me in the marsh
when the red-winged blackbird is not still.
Spring—and ease—will come quickly enough.

IV

That I vanished in a dark runnel
did not amuse you—there in the rustle
of our disquiet, this disquisition
on longing has left you abridged,
the anticipation of the spill
of my hair above you, once urgent
and appealing. As a child you used
to pluck the trumpets off the passionflower
and sip the stamen—nectaring, nectared,
by the pearl that forms at the thread's end.
The gaze of other women has turned me
into stone, you say, but you mean to turn
me into flesh and blood again.
I kid you not, you say. You do not kid.

V

In our last days, we'd agreed to be happy.
No striving. No ambition, a Gordian knot
of cats grooming on the bed, the odor
of cardamom, pork shanks braised in goat milk,
cleavage, nape, *gorge*—our tenderness falling
from the bone. We did not expect to survive
the winter: one mortal, one god, conjoining.
Even so, I cannot spare you, your china cup,
from breakage, your soul's eggshell—blue.
My arrows pierce through bone and will leave you
aching, my invitation always this: ache with me, my Soul.

At the Grand Central Oyster Bar

Down three flights of stairs,
pass through the glass doors beneath arches,
ancient entrances to tracks and commuter trains that no longer run,
buried where they burn in the ghost mine of the imagination,
under station and parkway.

There you'll find the stews and pan roasts,
peekytoe crab meat dressed in a colloidal chiffon of mayonnaise,
Ipswich clam sandwiches served with coleslaw and pickled tarter.

But let's talk about why you've come:
for oysters harvested from icy waters, the greats.
How far you've come to pay homage
at this shrine of Coffin Bays and Bluepoints,
Malpeques and Kumamotos, those deep-cupped thimbles
of flesh imported from Japan,
Belons, the French effetes,
and the Irish entrants,
the smooth-shelled native flats from Galway,
where to speak *oyster*
is to speak as if there were only one idiom
from Hrothgar to William Hague,
flesh fed by limestone and sandstone runoff
from Connemara to the Burren transported
by the sweet waters of conjoined rivers
and rocked gently in crates by true oystermen.
Shellfish have thrived here for 4000 years.

Order the indigenous Alaskan Windy Bays,
if you can get them,
harvested from a sedgy fissure by divers off Hawkins Island
with a knife twist that pries open the fiercely shut,
tricks the clamped, hasped hinge into yielding,

exposing the nacreous inner shell,
the pure, cold brine of oyster, that lightening sip.

Don't be late if you want a seat at the bar.
The doors open at 11:30.
That's where all the spirits dine.
in the bowels of a rocking ship,
singing a barcarole:
Seamus, Galway, Carolyn, Lucille.

And the money you'll pay with,
wherever it is mined, will be real silver.
The waiter will be slender,
his red hair a flame that leaps—
lighting up the bar.

Sophia

Every year, at this time,
the Mythic Children's Theater Wonder Float appears,
in a one-street parade wending past the mercantile

with its carousel of birdseye maple pipes, eau de Jean Nate,
and rack of BB guns, behind the VFW's khaki brigade
withering in the noonday heat, and a convoy of Gullwings and Skylarks,

cars that go up and down on double-helix hydraulic hoists,
past the derelict bar still boarded up like a one-eyed dog with its face
agape. (It's where you might have worked had you been born

into a different life.) Born into a different life, to different parents,
you might have toiled in the dark. That gutted building haunts you,
that missing eye: the corridor where the man with dirty hands almost raped.

Your gaze conscripted now by a ten-year-old nereid
flanked by a pair of nubile satyrs. She is luminous in her visitation,
anchoring her stillness in the sun, swathed in scarves of glint.

Maven of the dead, summer's retinue calls you:
Early Girls, Better Boys, Sweet 100s, dryads and nymphs
braceleted with hex beads.

Have you forgotten, in this desert at eight-thousand feet,
the farmers' markets and a farm-boy's kiss,
sea mandalas or the way the light strikes the breaking wave,

the breaking light of you, this season gold-fleeced like that fabled,
winged ram sired by Poseidon, born of Helios.

Summer summons you, child of Cassandra.
Dressed as summer or the sea, will you
come dressed as field of lavender or stark winter in her frozen sleeve?

The wave thins to sheer mirror.
You are ether and air and blue light.
In this vortex of wave, you think

that you, yourself, become spindrift and peak,
become transparent as these spirits of the sea,
phosphorescent with dripping luminosity.

Palace

As a God-struck child kneeling at the rail,
I believed more easily then
I saw the dove descending

to be fascicled in bread,
but then my eye grew inured,
and the Spirit did not visit.

Today, the snow fell differently,
and I untangled from the clapboard house
to feed the birds,

as ravenous as they
for the last red berries of pyracantha;
or was it the color

of their bodies against
the patches of snow
that pulled me toward them—

a red, bluer and more dull
than Castilian red or carmine—
the color of fall apples

cupped in a porcelain lotus.
I saw first gate, then palace,
then the legendary halls

appeared, shimmered in the sun.
Draped in diadem,
the Spirit hovered—unheavened,

homed in spalls of ice, trees rimed
with last year's fruit on straight, flagless stems,
semiquavers become quarter notes—

the sweet, shriven juice of all frost's shrivings—
fleet, brief—
suddenly made radiant.

Want

All the Buddhists in the world will tell you
that attachment is the source of suffering,
but what anchors you more than want,

hoars the skin
to silk-white ash and blush tincture
of Madder root,

smeary menstrual blood that chrisms
your thighs alizerin, stigmata of Persephone's
six seeds filched from Hades' banquet?

(Can you smell him now, after all these years,
the smell of his tobacco in wool?)
What is the origin of that word *mad*,

rubia tintorum, taproot that burrows
all the way to Hades?
You live there in that blaze's longing.

The cottonwoods wick
an amber talc of pollen suffusing the air,
light that cannot be rent.

Against the loden-green backdrop of kale,
the cottonwoods' cadmium fire
spells intensity's surrender, its not-yet, not-yet—

brilliant siren before the world turns dun,
ghost—dirty blonde of coyote.
And the heart, to be safe, leaves the body,

turns invisible, all shadow,
but continues to throw sparks,
yellow tinging ground fog's flocculent shroud.

Each year you wait for that light,
that light all at once,
with the martyrs your sung *O*

flung into the fire of ecstasy.
Who would want to extinguish
the flame that lit that match?

The Bookman

It is Easter Sunday, circa 1999, and snowing—a freak storm to be sure—in Tucson

where it *never* snows,

where the only sure wet comes in August

after a dry heat—

sky bent like the upper and lower limbs of a bow pinned back at full draw,

then let loose,

snatching up a white mop of Lhasa Apso in an instant—

the dog, the day,

swept away from its original intent

of hosannas,

buoyed by deluge and then dropped

unceremoniously

into what is.

This is history, the first time snow has fallen on Easter in a century,

sifting above a makeshift lean-to,   roofed but open

to a brick of baked caliche in Alden's backyard.

Hypnotized by great flakes, pillowy tufts, of white catching

in the erect spines of agave, falling even slower than disaster at the moment it unhinges,   we watch the crocheted lace of it fall,

trace asymmetrical knots in a pinewood table—

and await Alden's pies—Alden has promised to bake twenty of them,

but twenty has morphed into two—an apple and a berry, and a bottle of
          80 proof,

everyone gently tipsy, feeling the swirl of the pillowy tufts,

a gentle unmooring, not yet powerful enough to sweep us off our feet,

our toes still gripping the bottom of existence.

                              *

                                        Perhaps there was also a ham.

Perhaps Mark, perhaps Christine,

                                        perhaps Frances, were also there,

Perhaps memory is a fiction.

I can't remember *perhaps*.

If you wind the reel back,   there was still time.

Perhaps you can remember the time called *before*,   before

the all-you-can-do-is-see-yourself-in-a-split-second   where you know,

where you recognize that everything you've ever known   before

is going to be different after.

transfixed as you are, suspended in watching white flurries

> *waiting for pie in the promised land, Alden Border's*
> *promised land of twenty pies.*

*

This is years before I let go of everything I love—
the dog, the house, the agave, the table—before cancer
takes Alden with the quickness of a flash flood, before
I insist that my mother eat the host I have carried home
in a gold pix. *What am I to do with it if you refuse?* I say.
I want to know where to find you after you're dead.
I was so certain. This was my tragic flaw—
as if *my own* soul's status were not
in question, as if one were ever
in a position to judge one's own profligacy or faith.
I can't force her to take the Eucharist against her will, but I do.
I take her free will away. I *force* her,

> and the day settles into
> what is,
> and she's gone,

as in a child's cartoon: *bang, bang, dead—*

giant flakes as big as hands, falling even slower than disaster, the swirl of it as that

moment unhinges.

> *Where are they?*

*

In California, my parents are getting ready for bed, quail sifting secretly through the new riots of mustard, golden after the rains, all of it yellowing into a Sauternes end-of-day. My dutiful father, already dressed for bed, sets out the recycling bin for the Monday morning pickup as he always does every Sunday night—under the red pepper tree, its shower of pink peppercorns—

as we await pie, the scent
of the Easter pies baking.

*

Alden is a bookman.

The gift of a great bookman lies in his ability to pick out the right book for anyone. One can walk into a store and say, *I want a book for my uncle*, and he will come up with the perfect answer Dubay' s *The Evidential Power of Beauty* or Barthes' *A Lover's Discourse*. It's like a séance, his accuracy the bullseye of a great marksman—clairvoyant.

*

Having never driven a car

where it *never* snows, Alden knows

life's all about slow drift.

What counts is not how fast you
arrive but the weight of what you carry with you.

*

My father faints at the top of the driveway. The neighbors call 911 without telling my mother who doesn't know that the paramedics are on their way. She's washing dishes while smoking a cigarette and peers out the window just in time to catch the cherry-red flash of a fire truck, the paramedics dragging my father off to the hospital. She dons my father's gardening shoes, runs out the front door and trips, falling on the hard macadam of the driveway, breaking her hip and her wrist, and finally she says to my father those words he's been waiting to hear all his life: *Harry, Harry, what would I ever do without you? You're the great love of my life*, and they ride in the ambulance to the hospital hand in hand—this the denouement of a great love story, my mother in her bathrobe, the plush, blue one with its elbows worn to mesh. It bears the history of a long marriage, its cigarette burns and sewing needles and safety pins tucked into the lapel, threadbare but faithful, parts of it worn away into vanishing, as she will. The stone has rolled away from the tomb, a marriage far removed from its wedding day, marriage itself falling away from its original intention, like this day with its pie.

*

When Alden was pronounced dead,
Christine called to tell me that Alden
had regretted our last meeting. *It was fine*, I said,
but Alden must have told Christine
something different, a piece of gossip that I'll never hear.

Oh, honey, he'd say (he always called me *honey*),
you're just going through a hard patch.
But we didn't fall out, I said.

Why do I always think of the famed
Phantom Palace of Paris when I think of Alden?
I don't know, but Alden was like that.

He could make you imagine a world
polished into a high, crystal gloss
not separate from snow—

Hopkins' lovely asunder—all whiteout and drift,
the spirit spangled in the updraft and skein
of a whoosh swept skyward into attraction,

the flesh of it, this astonishing.
Alden looked at me with those hazel-brown eyes of his
and that eye-of-the-partridge sheen he gave off,

the way everything shimmering refracts
light just before it enters the tunnel
to meet the light on the other side,

travelling at the utmost speed one can manage,
slipping under the mesmer of peridot lights
and *bateaux mouche* on the water,

the reflecting pools of fountains at Trocadero,
a moment, a photon in squall, entering
that quick and native light,

and for the last time I ask Alden to name the perfect
book for me, expecting he'll say something like *Pedro Paramo*
or *The Joy of Man's Desiring*,

but no—he must know, he must be able to feel the tension—
like the limb-tips of a bow pulled back at full draw—
and he holds my face between his palms and says:

How to Pack a Suitcase.

NOTES

"After a Dark Tunnel, Uplift, Lift" shares resonances with Carolyn Forché's "Testimony of Light," and to the opening of her poem "Blue Hour. " Its open fieldwork and voice are after the poetry of 'Annah Sobelman who lost her six-year battle with cancer in 2017.

"Difficult Body" shares its title with Mark Wunderlich's poem from *The Anchorage* https://poets.org/poem/difficult-body and lines from Freud's essay "The Uncanny."

"Current Weather, Whether" was generated using aleatory methods inspired by John Cage.

"Codicil" employs the refrain "Write it" found in "Hunger Camp at Jaslo" by Wisława Szymborska as well as "Sun" by Michael Palmer.

"At the Grand Central Oyster Bar" pays homage to Richard Hugo's "Degrees of Gray in Philipsburg."

ACKNOWLEDGMENTS

Grateful acknowledgment is made to the editors of the following publications where these poems, some of which have been subsequently revised, originally appeared:

Lana Turner: "After a Dark Tunnel, Uplift, Lift"

Palette Poetry: "The Bookman"

Sporklet: "Sophia"

Under a Warm Green Linden: "Festina Lente," "Difficult Body," "Wabi Sabi"

Verse-Virtual: "Palace," "Sinistra"

Composition of *The Radiant* depended upon the enduring support of an essential core of companions, supporters and guides, Richard Howard, Carolyn Forché, Roberto J. Tejada, Nathan Filbert, Mark Wunderlich and my parents among them.

Special thanks to Josh Roark and the staff of *Palette Poetry* who awarded the "The Bookman" their Spotlight Award in 2018; and to Carmella Padilla and James McGrath Morris of NM Writers for a grant underwriting a portion of the expenses I incurred while writing *The Radiant*.

To my teacher, Alfred Corn, my gratitude for the gift of a rare and wonderful formation in prosody.

To Albert Goldbarth, Roberto J. Tejada, and Mark Wunderlich my thanks for taking time away from their own work to pen advance praise for *The Radiant*. It is no small labor.

To Taos photographer Geraint Smith for his splendid cover art <https://geraintsmith.com>

I wish to thank the many communities that have sustained me, especially The Community of Writers under the aegis of Galway Kinnell and Robert Hass's direction, the University of Wisconsin Institute of Creative Writing, the past participants of the Tupelo Conference in Truchas, New Mexico and finally the members of the generative, online poetry community I facilitate who have read and offered feedback on first drafts of many of these poems for a generosity and genuine devotion to the art. I wish especially to acknowledge Mickie Kennedy for his underwriting of several scholarships, as well as Sophie L. Cohen, C. W. Emerson, Will Barnes, Mary Barbara Moore, Frank Paino and Mike Burwell for their encouragement and support.

My thanks to Tupelo Press Editor-in-Chief Kristina Marie Darling and Managing Editor David Rossitter for their editorial expertise; and finally to Jeffrey Levine, this project's *sine qua non* and the publisher of Tupelo Press, I wish to express my enduring gratitude for his belief in *The Radiant* and for underwriting its publication in book form.

RECENT AND SELECTED TITLES FROM TUPELO PRESS

The Opening Ritual G.C. Waldrep

The Right Hand Christina Pugh

Called Back Rosa Lane

Landsickness Leigh Lucas

Green Island Liz Countryman

The Beautiful Immunity
Karen An-hwei lee

Small Altars Justin Gardiner

Country Songs for Alice Emma Binder

Asterism Ae Hee Lee

then telling be the antidote
Xiao Yue Shan

Therapon
Bruce Bond & Dan Beachy-Quick

membery Preeti Kaur Rajpal

How To Live Kelle Groom

Sleep Tight Satellite Carol Guess

THINE Kate Partridge

The Future Will Call You Something Else
Natasha Sajé

Night Logic Matthew Gellman

The Unreal City Mike Lala

Wind—Mountain—Oak: Poems of Sappho
Dan Beachy-Quick

Tender Machines J. Mae Barizo

Best of Tupelo Quarterly
Kristina Marie Darling, Ed.

We Are Changed to Dear at the Broken Place Kelly Weber

Why Misread a Cloud Emily Carlson

The Strings Are Lightning and Hold You
Chee Brossy

Ore Choir: The Lava on Iceland
Katy Didden and Kevin Tsang

The Air in the Air Behind It
Brandon Rushton

The Future Perfect: A Fugue
Eric Pankey

American Massif Nicholas Regiacorte

City Scattered Tyler Mills

Today in the Taxi Sean Singer

April at the Ruins Lawrence Raab

The Many Deaths of Inocencio Rodriguez
Iliana Rocha

The Lantern Room Chloe Honum

Love Letter to Who Owns the Heavens
Corey Van Landingham

Glass Bikini Kristin Bock

Tension : Rupture
Cutter Streeby, paintings Michael Haight

Afterfeast Lisa Hiton

Lost, Hurt, or in Transit Beautiful
Rohan Chhetri

Glyph: Graphic Poetry=Trans. Sensory
Naoko Fujimoto

The Pact Jennifer Militello

Nemerov's Door: Essays
Robert Wrigley

Ashore Laurel Nakanishi

Music for Exile Nehassaiu de Gannes

The Earliest Witnesses G.C. Waldrep

Master Suffering CM Burroughs

And So Wax Was Made & Also Honey
Amy Beeder

Sundays Thomas Gardner

Salat Dujie Tahat

The Age of Discovery Alan Michael Parker

Blood Feather Karla Kelsey

Fablesque Anna Maria Hong

Exclusions Noah Falck